Sea Witch

Story by Mike Lefroy
Illustrations by Liz Alger

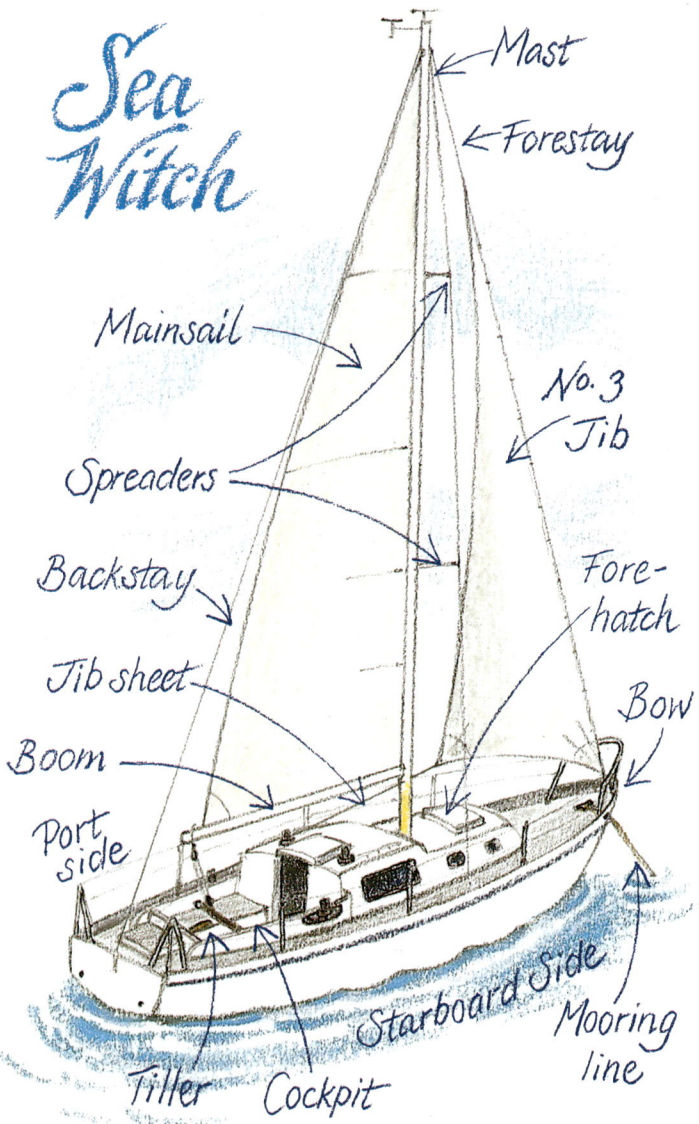

Sea Witch

Mast

Forestay

Mainsail

No. 3 Jib

Spreaders

Backstay

Fore-hatch

Jib sheet

Bow

Boom

Port side

Starboard Side

Tiller

Cockpit

Mooring line

Contents

Chapter 1	Collision!	4
Chapter 2	Adrift	8
Chapter 3	Out to Sea	17
Chapter 4	A Special Request	22
Chapter 5	Sea Rescue	26
Chapter 6	Night Surfing	30

Chapter 1
Collision!

"We won't be long... and don't use the tape deck, the batteries still aren't charging properly."

"Okay, we won't," said Kristie, throwing the bowline to her mother. Her twin brother, Jeremy, joined her on deck. They watched the little dinghy merge into the shoreline.

It was a perfect evening. The sea breeze still had a faint summer warmth. The twins sat on the cabin roof of *Sea Witch*, watching the sun thread its way through the pine trees and disappear behind the lighthouse.

They had been at the island for a week. This was their last evening before heading back to the mainland. A new school year was about to begin—their first year in high school.

"How about a game of cards?" Jeremy suggested. "I still haven't beaten you yet!"

The twins went down the stairs into the small but cosy cabin.

"It should be all right with one light," said Jeremy.

"Yeah, Mum and Dad are only worried about the tape deck because it uses more power," Kristie replied, expertly shuffling a pack of cards before dealing them out.

The twins sat huddled over the cards. This was serious. So serious that they didn't hear the *thump thump* of an approaching diesel engine.

Suddenly their world twisted violently. The cards spilt onto the cabin floor and the twins were jerked to their feet.

Kristie and Jeremy looked at each other in horror and then stumbled towards the stairs.

"Are you okay?" The anxious call came from a large fishing boat that was circling them.

"I... I think so?" Kristie stammered. The twins were shocked. They checked the deck. Everything seemed fine and, as the pitching of the yacht slowed to a gentle roll, they began to feel better.

"Yes... we're fine..." Jeremy called out. He looked across to the fishing boat that was now sweeping them with a bright searchlight.

"Sorry! We didn't see you. We hit your mooring buoy." The man at the end of the light was calmer now as he realised a major collision had been avoided. The light snapped off and once again the twins heard the powerful *thump thump* as the fishing boat headed out of the bay.

Chapter 2
Adrift

"We'd better stay on deck," said Kristie, who was still shaken. "Mum and Dad won't be long and we can shine the flashlight on the mast when we hear them coming."

The twins sat on the cabin roof and looked over towards the settlement. Jeremy shivered, but he wasn't cold. He was ready for an adult to come back and take charge.

"Jez…"

"What…?"

"Look over to the lighthouse. It seems to be going behind the hill," said Kristie.

"Don't be silly—lighthouses don't move. It's just the boat swinging on the mooring line," Jeremy said, remembering a time when he thought the boat was drifting out to sea. But it had only been the breeze changing direction and swinging the boat with it.

"No... look! Really!" Kristie was now standing by the mast, looking agitated.

Jeremy joined her. For nearly a minute, he surveyed the lighthouse and the lights at the settlement. Then he walked to the bow. Suddenly Jeremy swung back towards his sister, holding up a frayed piece of mooring line.

"Kristie! We are drifting! The fishing boat must have cut the line when it collided with our mooring buoy!"

"I'll try the engine," said Kristie, and she raced down the companionway to the control panel. Starting the engine was a simple task. It was one of the first jobs their father had let them do. Just make sure the gear lever is in neutral and push the button. But this time, instead of the *thump thump* of an engine starting, there was a tired bump of an engine being tickled by dying batteries.

Kristie and Jeremy looked at each other. Their night vision had returned after the glare of the fishing boat spotlight and they could sense in each other a growing fear. They looked across to the settlement again and then around the bay at the other boats.

"At least we're drifting away from danger," said Jeremy, at last.

"But not for long! The outer reef isn't too far away. See the marker?" Kristie pointed.

Kristie and Jeremy looked towards the flashing red light. Every flash across the water seemed to bring the marker closer to them.

"I'll get the jib," said Jeremy, with a new sense of urgency.

"Number 3 will do," Kristie called after him, slightly more confidently. The twins were good sailors and would soon be in their element.

The forehatch swivelled open and a sail bag appeared from below. Kristie heaved the sail onto the deck. She quickly clipped the sail onto the forestay as Jeremy attached the sheets and then scampered back to the cockpit. The team was working well.

"Okay, hoist away!" came Kristie's call.

Jeremy hauled swiftly on the rope. The flapping sail snaked upwards and the bow swung away from the wind as he fastened the rope. Kristie was now at the tiller, her eyes darting from the darkness in front of them to the flapping sail above.

Although Jeremy was half an hour older than Kristie, it had always been Kristie who took control. She always spoke first when they were introduced to strangers, and had always skippered the boats they sailed together.

Jeremy flicked three turns of rope around the winch and wound in the jib sheet. The sail was now in control. *Sea Witch* was picking up speed.

"We'll head away from the reef for a bit and then try and tack in to shore," said Kristie. She felt more confident now that the boat was sailing well and the red marker was receding.

★ ★ ★

"Why can't we see them yet?" asked Sophie, peering into the darkness from the dinghy.

"Try the flashlight," replied her husband. "See if you can read the number on that buoy."

"Number 42," said Sophie. "That's ours, isn't it?"

"Sure is... but where are they?" said Richard. There was a sudden urgency in his voice, and he quickened his stroke as they headed towards the lone mooring buoy.

★ ★ ★

"Isn't it beautiful out here?" said Jeremy, sitting beside Kristie, watching the waves. Kristie just nodded. She was enjoying the feel of the tiller and the sense of power that came with it.

The twins now felt full of confidence as *Sea Witch* reached across the smooth water at the mouth of the bay.

"Let's put up the mainsail, too," suggested Jeremy. "It'll help us get back in to the island and we'll go faster."

He leapt up nimbly and untied the mainsail cover. The sail flopped off the boom and he began to haul on the main rope.

The sail began sneaking upwards, but then it stopped suddenly.

"It's jammed!" shouted Jeremy, tugging on the rope.

Kristie fumbled for the flashlight by her feet and shone it up the mast. "Okay, I see the problem. The top's caught under the spreader. If we tack, the wind should blow it free."

Jeremy, crouching low, prepared to bring the jib around. Suddenly a gust of wind caught them and the boat heeled violently.

* * *

"There they are!" Sophie cried, pointing towards a distant light flashing on a flapping sail.

"What on earth are they doing putting the mainsail up?" said Richard. "They'll be out of the lee of the island any minute and into some real wind. We'll never catch them!"

Chapter 3

Out to Sea

"Pull it down, now!" yelled Jeremy, over the sound of the flogging sail. "It's free!"

Kristie grabbed the mainsail with both hands while angling her hip to keep the tiller in the centre of the boat. Jeremy helped her wrestle the sail back on board. They lashed it onto the boom with a spare piece of rope. The boat was now punching into a choppy sea and a building wind, both of which were combining to drive them slowly away from the island.

"We've got to tack and get back to the bay or we'll be stuck out here all night," called Kristie. Her voice wavered slightly. Their situation was getting very serious.

"Ready about? Lee-ho!" Kristie pushed the tiller away from her and the bow of the boat swung into the wind. *Sea Witch* paused, bucking head to wind for what seemed like an eternity. Then the boat began sailing backwards before finally falling back onto the old tack.

"Try again!" shouted Jeremy, winding in the jib so they could gather speed.

"Jez, don't let the jib go until the last moment," said Kristie with a calmness that surprised her. "That should push us around."

"Okay, let's go!" said Jeremy.

Kristie pushed the tiller more slowly. Jeremy waited until the jib was filling with wind from the other side before flicking off the turns on the winch. The sail smacked against the rigging and Jeremy dived for the other side of the boat to winch it home.

"Hard as you can!" yelled Kristie.

The twins sat beside each other on the windward rail, peering anxiously towards the dark shape of the island on their bow. A cloud slithered over the moon.

"The wind's swinging into the south," said Kristie, as they watched the lighthouse sweep a yellow beacon across the horizon. "We're not going to make it on this tack."

Kristie and Jeremy sat silently. Kristie concentrated hard to keep the boat sailing as close to the wind as possible. Jeremy watched the waves suddenly curl towards them from out of the blackness. Every so often, moonlight penetrated through the clouds and danced on the crests of the waves. In other circumstances, it would be an exhilarating sight.

★ ★ ★

"There's a strong wind warning that's just been posted by the Weather Bureau," said Ted Stevens, the island manager. Sophie and Richard took the news with silent, worried faces.

"Blast the engine batteries!" said Richard getting to his feet and pacing across the room.

"Is there any way we can contact them? Do they have a mobile phone?" asked Ted.

"It's in my pocket," said Sophie, angrily. Usually the phone was left on board if anyone was staying on the boat, but this time, for some reason, they had forgotten.

"Well, they're good sailors, your twins; they'll be fine," said Ted, hoping he sounded more confident than he felt.

Sophie nodded unconvincingly. Richard stopped pacing to look out the window across the bay.

Chapter 4
A Special Request

"Ready about?" called Kristie.

The boat surged up a steep wave as she pushed the helm down. The jib exploded with noise as Jeremy let the sheet go and it whipped itself across the boat. He winched in the shuddering rope with tired arms until he couldn't move it any more.

"How are we going now?" he called.

"We just seem to be sailing backwards and forwards without getting any closer to the island," said Kristie, with a tremor in her throat. She now had both hands on the tiller, trying hard to keep *Sea Witch* on course.

"I think we'd go better with the mainsail instead of the jib, but we can't do it in this wind," Kristie said. "Let's hope it dies down."

"I don't think it will," said Jeremy, looking up at the black clouds racing across the moon.

★ ★ ★

"Sea Rescue is setting off from the mainland in five minutes," said Ted to Sophie and Richard. "We can follow them on the radio. Any idea where the twins may be now?"

"Well, they were heading north when we saw them last," said Sophie, "but as soon as they were under control I'm sure they will have headed in towards the bay…"

"I can't see anything yet," said Richard, sweeping the horizon with Ted's binoculars.

★ ★ ★

"We'd better put the life jackets on. They'll make us warmer, anyway," Jeremy said as he sat shivering beside his sister.

He ducked down off the side of the boat, grabbed the flashlight from the cockpit floor and backed down the stairs into the cabin.

He quickly found the life jackets. He also grabbed two waterproof jackets and a couple of chocolate bars. Just as he began climbing out of the cabin, Jeremy saw his radio and grabbed it, too.

"Warm clothes, chocolate and music," he announced as he struggled back on deck.

The twins slipped into the jackets, clipped their safety lines onto the guard rail and peeled open the chocolate bars. Jeremy flicked the radio on. Their favourite radio station came pounding out.

"At least there's no problem with *these* batteries," he said, sitting beside Kristie.

"We're still not getting any closer," said Kristie, staring at the flash from the lighthouse.

★ ★ ★

"The radio!" said Sophie, suddenly. "I bet they're listening to the radio."

Ted and Richard turned to her quizzically.

"We can send a message to them through the radio!"

Sophie quickly rang the radio station. "Hello?" she said anxiously. "I'd like to make a special request."

Chapter 5

Sea Rescue

"The wind's up to 35 knots in gusts now," said Mack Hall to Ernie Rigg, at the wheel.

Ernie Rigg nodded in reply. As skipper of the Sea Rescue vessel *Endeavour*, he'd been in much stronger winds and heavier seas than these—but never trying to track down thirteen-year-old twins in charge of a runaway yacht. He knew both he and the twins were in for a tough night.

"If they've managed to set the sails, their parents reckon they'll head for the island," said Ernie. "We'll try a grid search pattern between the point and the outer reef light."

"It's going to be difficult," sighed Mack. "Their navigation lights are out."

★ ★ ★

After completing what felt like their hundredth tack, the twins huddled together. Jeremy was on the tiller, giving Kristie a rest. The cold began to seep through their jackets.

They knew their situation was now extremely serious. After seemingly getting closer to the lighthouse, they were now clearly losing sight of it. The wind and seas were pushing them further away from the island.

"Our next request is a very special one for two young sailors on the high seas tonight. Hello to Kristie and Jeremy, from Richard and Sophie—your parents, if you've forgotten!

"They want you to know that the Sea Rescue ship **Endeavour** is heading your way. They want you to fire a flare and shine your flashlight on the sail so **Endeavour** can see you. While you're doing all that, here's a special song for you…"

Jeremy and Kristie just looked at each other in disbelief, more out of shock that their parents were listening to *their* station than from the message itself.

★ ★ ★

"A flare!" cried Richard, putting down the binoculars. "Did you see that?"

The radio crackled into life. "*Endeavour* to Ted Stevens... Sea Rescue ship *Endeavour* calling Ted Stevens..."

Ted Stevens grabbed the handset, "Reading you loud and clear *Endeavour*... go ahead..."

"We have a bearing on the flare... about three nautical miles north-west," replied Ernie Rigg. "We're heading that way now..."

Sophie and Richard smiled at each other for the first time that evening. They huddled around the radio, waiting for the next report.

Chapter 6

Night Surfing

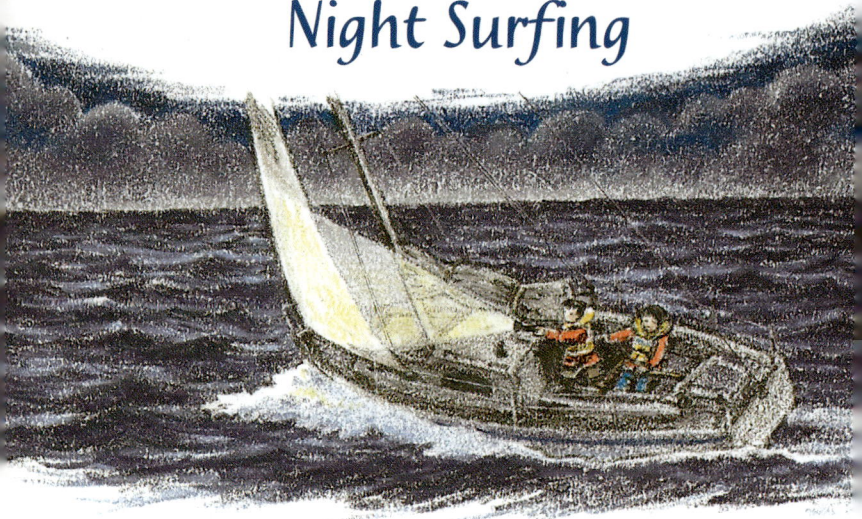

"Over there!" cried Kristie, tugging at Jeremy's jacket. Jeremy swept the flashlight up and down the sail with renewed vigour.

"And here's another message for our two sailors Kristie and Jeremy. Thanks for the flares... I thought they went out of fashion in the 70s... Anyway... when the good ship Endeavour reaches you, they want you to turn and follow them, if you can. They'll lead you back to the Port Marina. Flash your light on and off to let Endeavour know you've got this message."

"Okay, Ernie... I can see them... just off our port bow..." said Mack to his skipper. "They're sailing well," he added, admiringly.

"And they're flashing at us, so they're ready to follow," said Ernie. "I'll radio the island and let them know."

Without taking his eyes off *Sea Witch*, Ernie reached across the wheel and picked up the radio handset.

"Sea Rescue ship *Endeavour*... Ted, we have them alongside and we're heading home..."

Kristie tugged the tiller towards her as Jeremy eased the jib sheet. *Sea Witch* wallowed in the trough of a wave, but was soon on course and surfing down the face of the steepening seas. Kristie clutched the tiller with both hands and locked her eyes on *Endeavour*.

"It's time to sign off now. Thanks for all the great requests. And to our intrepid sailors, Kristie and Jeremy, we hear you're engaged in a little night surfing. Hang in there!"

But Jeremy and Kristie didn't hear the radio. They were whooping with an equal mixture of fear and exhilaration as *Sea Witch* thundered in a shower of spray towards the bright lights of the Port Marina.